THE LIBRARY OF WHY?

Why Did the Dinosaurs Become Extinct?

Marian B. Jacobs, Ph.D

The Rosen Publishing Group's
PowerKids Press™
New York

For my grandsons, Carlos and Gianni.

Published in 1999 by The Rosen Publishing Group, Inc.
29 East 21st Street, New York, NY 10010

First Edition

Book Design: Danielle Primiceri

Photo Credits: pp. 4, 11, 12 © Corbis-Bettmann; p. 7 © Dewitt Jones/Corbis; p. 8 © Jonathan Blair/Corbis, © Ron Thomas/FPG International; pp. 15, 22 © Jonathan Blair/Corbis; p. 16 © Corbis; p. 19 © 1997 Digital Vision Ltd.; p. 20 © Michael Agiolo/ International Stock.

Jacobs, Marian B.
      Why did the dinosaurs become extinct? / by Marian B. Jacobs.
          p.   cm. — (The library of why?)
      Includes index.
      Summary: Discusses scientific theories regarding the disappearance of the dinosaurs including disease, climate changes, starvation, and a meteor collision.
      ISBN 0-8239-5276-2
      1. Dinosaurs—Juvenile literature. 2. Extinction (Biology)—Juvenile literature.   [1. Dinosaurs.
2. Extinctions (Biology).] I. Title. II. Series
QE862.D5J288   1998
567.9—dc21   97-48449
                                                                                                        CIP
                                                                                                        AC

Manufactured in the United States of America

Contents

What Is a Theory?

Dinosaurs were animals that lived millions of years ago. They were much like the reptiles that live today. The dinosaurs lived for about 150 million years all over the world. Then they became **extinct** (ik-STINKT). We don't know exactly what happened to the dinosaurs, so scientists have come up with many **theories** (THEER-eez) to explain their disappearance. A theory is a group of ideas that explain something. For a theory about dinosaur extinction to work, it must explain why other plants and animals died out at the same time.

◀ *There were many different kinds of dinosaurs living on Earth millions of years ago.*

What Do Fossils Tell Us?

Almost everything we know about dinosaurs comes from their **fossils** (FAH-sulz). When dinosaurs died, their bodies were buried under mud and sand. As millions of years passed, the mud, sand, bones, teeth, footprints, and plant and tree remains, became rock. These rocks are fossils.

Scientists study fossils and the ground in which they are found to figure out how old they are. They study these fossils to learn about the time when dinosaurs lived and to form theories about why they became extinct.

Fossils can be hard to find because they are buried deep in the earth. ▶

Was It a Change in Climate?

One theory about how the dinosaurs died says that a quick change from warm weather to very cold weather killed them. Animals such as reptiles and dinosaurs are cold-blooded and need to sit in the sun to keep themselves warm. Very cold weather would harm them.

This theory does not work because other reptiles living at the time of the dinosaurs, such as crocodiles and turtles, did **survive** (ser-VYV). Now scientists think the weather changed slowly. Dinosaurs had time to move to warmer places or to **adapt** (uh-DAPT) to changes.

◀ *The weather affects all the plants and animals on Earth.*

Did Mammals Eat All the Dinosaur Eggs?

Fossilized dinosaur eggs found by scientists show that dinosaurs gave birth to their young by laying eggs. These eggs were food for **mammals** (MA-mulz). Mammals were small animals that hunted at night when they were not easily seen by dinosaurs. Did the mammals attack the dinosaur eggs and eat them all? Scientists do not think this theory works. The mammals probably were not able to eat *all* the dinosaur eggs. This theory also doesn't explain why many **species** (SPEE-sheez) of plants became extinct as well.

Scientists believe that these dinosaur eggs are about 100 million years old! ▶

Were Their Brains too Small?

As dinosaurs **evolved** (ee-VOLVD) their bodies got bigger but their brains stayed small. Apatosaurus was the size of a six-story building, but its brain was the size of an orange. How could such a small brain work with such a large body? Did its small brain mean that Apatosaurus wasn't smart enough to survive?

This is not a good theory because some dinosaurs with small brains survived for 150 million years. And not all dinosaurs had small brains. But all the dinosaurs died.

◄ *What most people know as Brontosaurus is now called Apatosaurus.*

Did Dinosaurs Die From Disease?

Another theory says that a terrible illness killed all the dinosaurs. As some dinosaurs got sick and died, meat-eating dinosaurs ate them. Then the meat-eating dinosaurs got sick. In this way, the illness spread across the world.

This is not a good theory because one illness would probably not harm every kind of dinosaur. How did crocodiles and turtles survive? Also, this does not explain the extinction of plants. A dinosaur-killing illness would not kill plants.

Though disease may have spread easily, one disease probably would not have killed all the dinosaurs. ▶

Did All the Dinosaurs Starve?

Plant-eating dinosaurs needed hundreds of pounds of plant food every day to survive. They ate mostly soft plants called ferns.

Near the end of the dinosaurs' time, these plants died out. New species of plants began to grow. Some scientists think that some dinosaurs couldn't chew these new plants. Then these plant-eating dinosaurs would have **starved** (STARVD). The meat-eating dinosaurs who ate the plant-eating dinosaurs would have died next because they had no food. But this theory still can't explain the extinction of other plants and animals.

The extinction of some plants and the growth of new ones was probably not harmful enough to kill all the dinosaurs.

Did a Supernova Kill the Dinosaurs?

A supernova is an exploding star. When a star explodes, it releases a blast of light, heat, and **radiation** (RAY-dee-AY-shun). Millions of years ago, a supernova may have covered Earth with deadly radiation. It would have killed many plants and animals right away. Others would have died later.

If this happened, scientists would find **radioactive** (RAY-dee-oh-AK-tiv) material in the rocks with dinosaur fossils. But this material has not been found.

The supernova theory was the first one that said something from outer space may have killed the dinosaurs. ▸

Did a Meteor Kill the Dinosaurs?

During a study of **sedimentary** (sed-ih-MEN-tree) rock, scientists found a rare heavy metal called **iridium** (eer-RIH-dee-um). The iridium was found in a layer of rock formed during the same time as the extinction of the dinosaurs.

Iridium is hardly ever found on Earth's surface. It is usually found in **meteors** (MEE-tee-orz) and other rocks from outer space that have landed on Earth. Scientists think that a large iridium-rich meteor smashed into Earth. Imagine what a crash that would be!

◄ *Meteors fly through space all the time. In fact, shooting stars are actually meteors.*

What Happens if a Meteor Hits?

A meteor traveling very fast would have crashed into Earth very hard. The crash would have created huge clouds of dust and rock that would have blocked out the light of the sun. These clouds would have hung in the air for many years. They would have stopped plants from growing.

The crash would have created a huge **crater** (KRAY-ter), caused earthquakes, caused volcanic eruptions, and forest fires. This theory is still being studied by scientists today. So far, it best explains the extinction of the dinosaurs and plants from long ago.

Glossary

adapt (uh-DAPT) To change because of new conditions.

crater (KRAY-ter) A hole in the ground shaped like a bowl.

evolve (ee-VOLV) To develop or change.

extinct (ik-STINKT) When something no longer exists.

fossil (FAH-sul) The remains of something that have turned to rock.

iridium (eer-RIH-dee-um) A rare heavy metal often found in meteors.

mammal (MA-mul) An animal that is often covered with hair, gives birth to live young, and feeds milk to its young.

meteor (MEE-tee-or) A rock from outer space.

radiation (RAY-dee-AY-shun) Rays of light, heat, or energy that spread outward from something.

radioactive (RAY-dee-oh-AK-tiv) Something that gives off radiation.

sedimentary (sed-ih-MEN-tree) Rock that is formed by gravel, sand, silt, or mud that is left behind by water or wind.

species (SPEE-sheez) A similar group of plants or animals.

starve (STARV) To die from lack of food and drink.

survive (ser-VYV) To keep living.

theory (THEER-ee) An idea or group of ideas that tries to explain something.

Index